W9-BPM-431

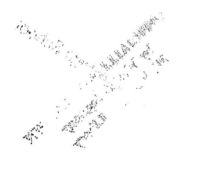

TICK-BORNE ILLNESSES

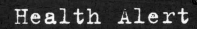
TICK-BORNE ILLNESSES

L. H. Colligan

Marshall Cavendish
Benchmark
New York

With thanks to Raymond J. Dattwyler MD, Professor of Medicine and Microbiology/Immunology, New York Medical College, for his expert review of the manuscript.

Marshall Cavendish Benchmark
99 White Plains Road
Tarrytown, New York 10591-5502
www.marshallcavendish.us

Library of Congress Cataloging-in-Publication Data

Colligan, L. H.
Tick-borne illnesses / by L.H. Colligan.
p. cm. — (Health alert)
Summary: "Provides comprehensive information on the causes, treatment, and history of tick-borne illnesses"—Provided by publisher.
Includes index.
ISBN 978-0-7614-2914-2
1. Tick-borne diseases—Juvenile literature.   I. Title.
RA641.T5C65 2009
616.9'68—dc22

2007038517

Front cover: Magnified view of a deer tick
Title page: Lone star ticks, showing top and underside views
Photo Research by Candlepants Incorporated
Cover Photo: Volker Steger / Peter Arnold Inc.

The photographs in this book are used by permission and through the courtesy of:
Corbis: Rob Howard, 8; Cdc/Phil, 23; W. Perry Conway, 27; Raymond Gehman, 34; Naturfoto Honal, 35; Layne Kennedy, 37; Tony Kurdzuk/Star Ledger, 51; Creasource, 56. Alamy Images: Imagestate, 10; Bubbles Photolibrary, 45. Animals Animals: David M. Dennis, 12. Photo Researchers Inc.: Eye Of Science, 5, 17, 31, 43; Dan Suzio, 13; Scott Camazine, 18; Kenneth M. Highfill, 19; Spl, 20; Larry Mulvehill, 21; Science Source, 28; Sinclair Stammers, 33. Minden Pictures: Michael Durham, 14; Ingo Arndt, 16. Getty Images: 15; 3d4medical.Com, 41; Todd Gipstein, 49. PhotoTakeUSA.com: Luis M. De La Maza, Ph.D. M.D., 29, 3. AP Images: Ap Photo/Thomas Wright, Ho, 39; Ap Photo/Centers For Disease Control, James Gathany, 24. Rocky Mountain Laboratories/National Institute of Allergy and Infectious Diseases: 42. Shutterstock: Sebastian Kaulitzki, 54.

Editor: Joy Bean
Publisher: Michelle Bisson
Art Director: Anahid Hamparian

Printed in Malaysia
6 5 4 3 2 1

CONTENTS

Chapter 1	What Is It Like to Have a Tick-Borne Illness?	6
Chapter 2	What Is a Tick-Borne Illness?	12
Chapter 3	The History of Tick-Borne Illnesses	36
Chapter 4	Living with a Tick-Borne Illness	48
	Glossary	58
	Find Out More	61
	Index	63

WHAT IS IT LIKE TO HAVE A TICK-BORNE ILLNESS?

After a great summer, the school year did not get off to the best start for fourteen-year-old Matt. A few days before the first day of school, he felt tired and had a dull headache off and on. Then, just before school started, Matt woke up feeling as though his body were on fire. His mother felt his forehead and immediately took his temperature. It was quite high: 104 degrees Fahrenheit (40 degrees Celsius). Not only that, but Matt's headache was much worse and constant. Despite his high fever, he also had the chills. His mother said she would call their family doctor to see what might be going on.

All Matt wanted to do was sleep. His older brother said he was probably worn out after working all summer as a junior camp counselor. Those little kids could really run him around. There was always one or two of them out sick. Matt thought he probably just had some kind of bug. His parents were not so sure about that. He suddenly seemed unusually sick. Besides the fever and ongoing headache, his muscles began to ache something awful. Soon he developed terrible stomach pains, and he started to vomit. His mother remembered reading about an eight-year-old girl who had died the summer before from something that began with the same symptoms Matt had. It turned out that the girl had been bitten by a **tick** that carried **Rocky Mountain spotted fever (RMSF)**.

Matt's mother called and left a message for the doctor. She and her husband looked up the symptoms on the Internet. Matt did not have a rash, but he did have many of the other symptoms of RMSF. His mother also learned that there were more and more cases each year in North Carolina, where they lived.

Matt felt too sick and confused to remember whether a tick had bitten him recently. But it was possible. He and the other counselors had one last campout in the mountains less than two weeks before his symptoms began. They had all slept in lean-to shelters, and hauled in chopped wood for the nightly campfires from a nearby woodpile.

During the day, everyone hiked the mountain trails. Matt and the other counselors made sure their campers wore long pants tucked into their socks and put on insect repellent and sunscreen every day. Matt had shown the young campers how to stash their food in bear bags that were hauled up trees so

Anyone can enjoy the outdoors and avoid tick-borne illnesses by wearing long pants, using insect repellent, and checking for ticks after being outside.

animals would not get into the food. There was no shortage of chipmunks, ground squirrels, and mice scurrying around the lean-tos. Matt and the other counselors told their young charges not to keep even a cookie crumb in the lean-to. They did not want to attract animals during the night.

Matt's parents knew from reading about ticks that there was no way their son would remember being bitten by one a couple of weeks ago. Ticks bite in such a way that victims do not feel the bite. After a tick fills up on a victim's blood, it drops off. Any diseases it may have carried would cause trouble later on—days and weeks after the tick had crawled away. That could be what was happening to Matt now.

Matt's parents checked his stomach and back for a rash again, but he did not have one. But even without a rash, Matt could still have RMSF. Rashes for some tick-borne illnesses did not always break out right away. When the doctor called back, Matt's mother said she was worried. This did not seem like the kind of flu both boys had had over the years. She mentioned that Matt had spent all summer working outdoors and had recently been camping. She asked whether it was possible he had a tick-borne illness. The doctor told Matt's family to come in the following morning.

Matt's fever, headache, and stomach pains were worse the next day. He was confused and miserable. His eyes were red. He buried his head under his sweatshirt hood even though he was burning up. When the doctor saw Matt, she immediately checked his ankles, then his wrists. "The rash is just starting to form," she said. "By tomorrow that rash will probably be spread all over. It is very possible that Matt has Rocky Mountain spotted fever. I am not going to wait for test results. It can take a

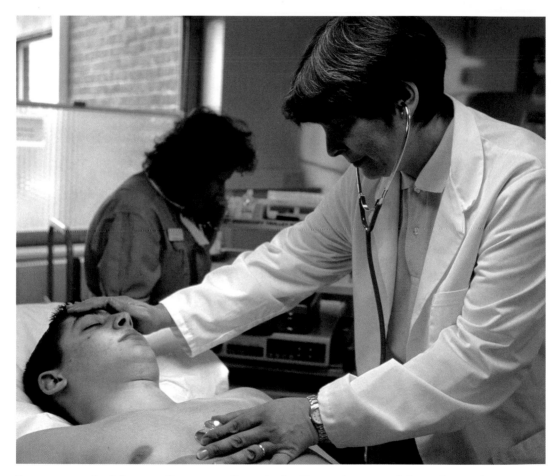

Teenagers and adults usually recover from Rocky Mountain spotted fever faster than children do. Anyone with sudden fever, severe headache, and a developing rash should seek medical care immediately.

long time to confirm them. I am glad you all came in. Matt needs to start **antibiotic** treatment immediately."

The doctor gave Matt's parents a prescription for an antibiotic called tetracycline. She said his outcome would likely be a good one. The eight-year-old girl who had died of kidney failure due to Rocky Mountain spotted fever had not received treatment until nearly two weeks after her first symptom appeared. The doctor reassured Matt and his family that taking the full ten-day course of medication should make him better.

Matt went home and started taking the medication. He felt better every day, but he started the new school year several days later than everyone else. After finishing all his medication, he felt almost back to normal. He never did remember getting bitten by a tick that summer. It could have happened on one of the campouts. But it also could have happened in the woods in back of his house where he and his brother liked to go and throw sticks into the water for their dog to fetch. Sometimes they ran around barefoot and in shorts back there. Maybe a tick had bitten Matt then.

2

WHAT IS A TICK-BORNE ILLNESS?

Tick-borne illnesses are diseases that are spread by tiny blood-feeding organisms called ticks. This happens when the tick feeds on an infected animal, called a **host**. The tick then carries that **infection** to another animal. Sometimes, the tick's next host turns out to be a human passing through a tick-infested area.

For ticks, only one kind of food is on the menu—blood from a **vertebrate**, an animal with a bony spine. More than eight hundred tick types, or species, live on land throughout the world. They thrive

Ticks, such as this American dog tick, feast on the blood of many animals with spines—birds, mice, rats, cattle, sheep, camels, goats, bears, reptiles, deer, cats, dogs—and humans.

wherever there are vertebrates, from grasslands and forests to mountains and deserts. Ticks spend 90 percent of their time living in such **habitats** and the other 10 percent attached to animals.

Ticks may look like insects, but belong to a biting group of spineless invertebrates called **arachnids**. This group includes spiders, scorpions, and mites. Despite having hundreds of species, ticks have only two types of body coverings: soft and hard. Soft ticks, called *Argasidae*, have soft, leathery bodies. They lack the hard plate covering of hard ticks. Soft ticks are fast eaters that can take in a full blood meal in twenty to

Ticks have been pestering animals, reptiles, and birds with their bloodthirsty ways for about 90 million years.

seventy minutes. They live in burrows, nests, woodpiles, and under porches and roofs where birds and small animals live. Soft ticks transmit most of the diseases they carry to animals and birds. However, they can cause **tick-borne relapsing fever (TBRF)** in humans who encounter them.

Hard ticks, called *Ixodidae*, cause most tick-borne illnesses in humans. They feed slowly. They live on the ground in more open and varied habitats than soft ticks do. Hard tick hideouts may include the undersides of grasses and leaves, or they may

A hard tick may feed on the blood of an animal for as long as thirteen days. During that time the host animal is usually unaware that a tick is attached.

live in sand, dirt, or dust that hosts kick up while passing through. Once they attach to a host, hard ticks may feed for nearly two weeks. Unfortunately for the host, this gives the hard tick a great deal of time to deliver diseases it may have picked up from its previous host. Ticks may also carry more than one disease, which can cause multiple infections in the host.

Both soft and hard ticks experience three life-cycle forms after they hatch from eggs: **larva, nymph**, and adult. In order for a tick to grow from one stage to the next, it must consume a large blood meal. Without it, the tick will die. A blood meal is important in mating as well. For many types of ticks, males will mate with adult females only after the females have finished feeding. Ticks can live for an entire year on a single feeding of blood.

To the human eye, ticks hardly look capable of sickening a large human, a flying bird, a hopping toad, or a four-legged animal, let alone killing some with the diseases they spread.

Both the adult tick (upper left) and nymph tick (bottom right) swell up to many times their normal size after feeding on blood.

At first glance, ticks do not seem to have much going for them. They lack antennae that insects use to sense smells, sounds, moisture, and temperature. Ticks do not have wings to fly. A tick crawls too slowly to chase down a host, so it must wait for one to show up in its habitat. However, when it comes to spreading disease, ticks are second only to mosquitoes as **vectors.**

The disease-spreading process begins when a tick vector drinks blood from an infected animal. The blood may contain harmful disease-causing **pathogens** such as certain **bacteria.** Or the host animal's blood may be infected with a harmful **virus.** These harmful particles multiply when they invade a host's cells,

Ticks that sense a host approaching will climb a leaf, a stalk of grass, or a stick and wave their barbed, hooked legs to catch a ride when the host passes by.

causing illness in the host. Sometimes ticks attach themselves to animals infested with **parasites**. These organisms hitch a ride inside ticks to the next host. Ticks deposit the parasites in the host animal's blood while feeding. When the tick drops off, the parasites stay behind. They survive by stealing nutrients from the host, making it sick. This can all take place because of a creature about the size of a pencil mark. How do tiny ticks get away with causing so much damage?

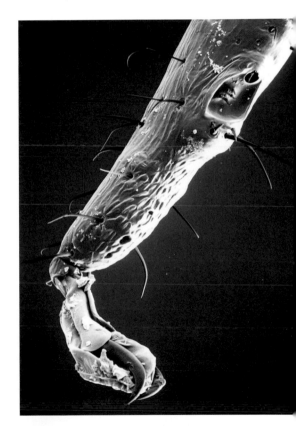

Nearly every part of a tick's body is devoted to one purpose—finding and drinking blood. Spreading disease just happens in the process. To find a meal, the tick has one incredible body part, called the Haller's organ, located on one of its legs. This tiny organ can sense that a host is approaching. This information excites the tick, which then exhibits **questing** behavior as it readies itself to climb on the host. (Soft ticks wait for the host to enter the tick's nesting spaces.) Once on board a host, the tick's Haller's organ keeps working. It senses heat and odors on the host's skin and

The dent on this tick's leg shows its Haller organ, which senses a potential host's odors, body temperature, breath, vibrations, as well as changes in air currents when a host is moving nearby.

signals good feeding spots. On birds and four-legged animals, this suitable feeding place will be located on the skin, deep within the animals' feathers, fur, scales, or hair. On humans, ticks often attach to lower limbs or in hidden areas of the body, such as the groin, or skin folds. But ticks will sometimes travel up to the head where they attach behind a person's ears or on the scalp. When a tick finds a suitable feeding spot, it drills itself into the host and remains attached until it is full of blood.

The Haller's organ is not the only feature suited to ticks' blood-drinking ways. Despite consuming infected blood, ticks usually do not get sick from the organisms they carry. A tick's **immune system** produces substances that kill off many of the infectious organisms it may carry. Some tick cells can even surround an invading organism to keep it from getting into the tick's tissues.

However, many animals that ticks bite are not so lucky. They do get sick. In a human, **symptoms** of most tick-borne illnesses usually begin with

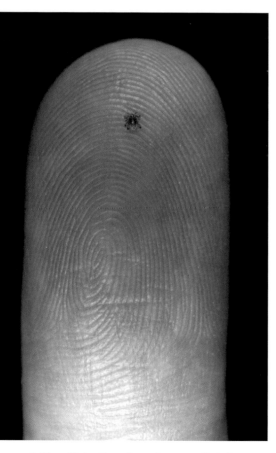

A tiny tick, the size of a pencil dot, can carry multiple tick-borne illnesses, including encephalitis.

a fever. This is a sign that the person's body is heating up to fight off the tick-borne disease. Other symptoms may include headache, muscle and joint pain, rashes, bleeding, loss of appetite, nausea, and, rarely, fatal paralysis. Unfortunately, the host does not usually experience these symptoms right away. That is because many ticks have something else going for them. Many ticks produce a numbing anesthetic in their saliva that they inject into the host. This substance keeps the host from feeling the bite and the tick can dig in without the likelihood of being brushed away.

TICKS AND DISEASE

Nothing happens in humans or animals if a tick that bites them is not carrying any pathogens. Of all the ticks that do carry disease, only a small percentage of them bite humans. Ticks prefer other hosts to humans. These may include birds and small ground animals such as mice, chipmunks, and squirrels. They also prefer to feed on grazing animals such as cattle, sheep, deer, and goats.

The tick feeding on this rabbit's ear may go on to infect the next host with diseases the rabbit may be carrying, including tularemia.

Digging In

A hiker is passing through a grassy meadow on an early September day. The hiker's movements excite the black-legged hard ticks lurking on the ground. They have not tasted blood for more than a year. Many of the ticks climb blades of grass exactly where they sense the hiker will be walking by. As soon as the hiker brushes against the grasses, several ticks climb on. One female tick makes it past the hiker's boots and socks. She finds a feeding spot on the hiker's leg. The other ticks fall to the ground where they will wait for another host to pass by, perhaps a chipmunk.

The tick works quickly on the leg of its human host. It digs in for its meal with a hooked, drill-like mouthpart called a **hypostome**. On this particular day, the tick is carrying corkscrew-shaped bacteria called **spirochetes**. The tick picked up these spirochetes when it fed on a field mouse's infected blood the year before. Now the spirochetes will get into the hiker's skin at the bite site. Later, they may travel through the host's bloodstream into other organs, the joints, heart, or brain.

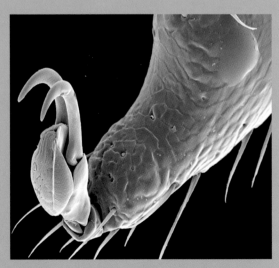

A tick's mouthpart attaches itself and also secretes a cement-like saliva to keep itself glued to a host during feeding.

The tick also injects chemicals into its host so it can continue feeding: Aside from the numbing substance it releases, which prevents the host's immune system from recognizing the hungry invader feeding on its leg, another substance keeps the hiker from feeling itchy or getting a rash right away. Still another substance prevents the hiker's blood from clumping into a scab where the tick has attached itself. All the while, spirochete bacteria are flowing freely from the tick to the host's blood and begin invading the host's tissues and organs. While all this is happening, the hiker has no idea a tick is gorging on his blood.

The tick stays attached to the hiker for nearly two weeks, undiscovered. It is loaded with blood. Finally, it secretes yet another substance. This one dissolves the hardened saliva that anchored it to the host, and the tick drops off. Meanwhile, inside the hiker's body, the **incubation period** for illness is over. The hiker starts to feel sick nearly a week after the tick detaches. He has a low-grade fever and a mild but constant headache. He notices a pink rash on his thigh that spreads out in a circle on his leg over several days.

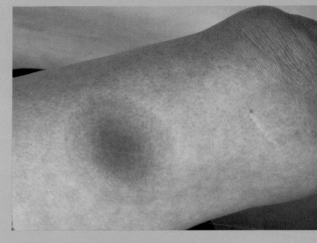

Not everyone who gets Lyme disease develops an expanding red rash, but many do. Anyone with a rash, fever, and headache should see a doctor.

The hiker goes to the doctor. The doctor asks whether a tick could have bitten him. The hiker vaguely remembers his hike a couple of weeks back. After the doctor notes the hiker's symptoms, she has a likely diagnosis. She says he probably has the tick-borne illness **Lyme disease.** She takes a blood sample for testing, but says the tests do not always provide a definite answer, and results can take some time. She writes a prescription for an antibiotic. This medication should clear up the symptoms. She tells the patient to make another appointment to see her again in about three weeks, when the hiker has finished taking all the medication. The doctor wants to make sure the symptoms have gone away completely.

The usual sequence for many ticks is first to feed on mice as larvae, then on a four-legged animal or human at the nymph stage, and then on another four-legged animal or human at the adult stage. In order for a tick to feed on a human, however, that human must be passing through tick territory during tick feeding season—usually from April or May to September. The people at greatest risk of being bitten and developing a tick-borne illness are those who spend a great deal of time outdoors. This group includes farmers, ranchers, forest rangers, construction and road workers, outdoor athletes, and hikers.

Ticks carry diseases wherever they live around the world. In North America, ticks cause Lyme disease, Rocky Mountain spotted fever, **ehrlichiosis**, **tularemia**, tick-borne relapsing fever, and **babesiosis**, among other diseases that are very rare.

LYME DISEASE

The black-legged hard tick is one of the troublemaking vectors that spreads Lyme disease. This is the most common tick-borne illness in North America and in Europe. Lyme disease, which gets its name from a town in Connecticut where there was an outbreak of the disease in children in 1975, makes up about 90 percent of infections that tick vectors spread in the United States. Fortunately, just 3 to 5 percent of people bitten by the kinds of ticks that carry Lyme disease actually develop the disease. However, the numbers add up. Between 1980 and early

Black-legged ticks, carriers of Lyme disease, usually feed more frequently on small and large grazing animals than on humans.

fall 2007, forty-nine states reported a total of 299,019 cases of Lyme disease to the United States Centers for Disease Control. Experts believe, however, that actual cases of Lyme disease are thirteen to fifteen times higher than that since most cases do not get reported. This means there have probably been nearly 2 million cases of Lyme disease since 1980. Unfortunately, people who get Lyme disease once can get it again if another infected tick bites them. Ninety percent of Lyme disease cases occur in the northeast, northern California, and the upper Midwest. These are areas where there are large populations of white-footed mice and white-tailed deer—ticks' favorite hosts.

The majority of human hosts for black-legged ticks are males over the age of twenty-nine who spend time outdoors, working or playing sports. Children and teens up to age fifteen who live, play, and participate in sports in tick-infested areas make up another large group at high risk of getting Lyme disease. Humans who get the disease develop it after having been bitten by a black-legged tick that has fed on one or more of the 119 species hosts infected with the spirochete bacteria.

One of the first signs that someone may have Lyme disease is a low-grade fever and, in 70 to 80 percent of the cases, an expanding red, painless rash that the victim may get days or weeks after being bitten. The rash is usually three or four inches in diameter when the doctor first sees it. By the time these symptoms develop, the tick has detached. Most of the time, the tick-bite victim does not recall being bitten. If the patient is treated with appropriate antibiotics for at least two to four weeks, the symptoms usually clear up. Some doctors recommend injections of high-dose antibiotics for several weeks.

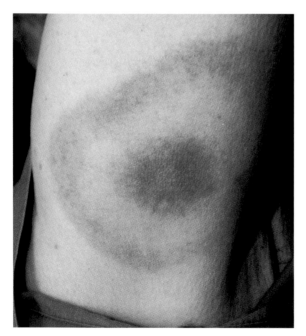

The Lyme disease rash sometimes appears as an expanding bull's eye, though it is commonly just red.

Lyme Disease Symptoms

Stage	Incubation	Possible Symptoms
First stage	several days to several weeks	expanding rash headaches fever neck stiffness tiredness joint and muscle pain
Second stage	one week to several months	joint pain and swelling slow heart beat meningitis possible face paralysis
Third stage	months to years	heart problems arthritis mental confusion eye infections

For people who do not get adequate treatment early on, other symptoms may develop. Such patients may suffer facial paralysis, arthritis, eye infections, heart problems, weakened immune systems, and **neurological** problems that cause mental confusion. These symptoms may last for years. Such patients should see a specialist in Lyme disease and other tick-borne illnesses. They will need to undergo intensive testing to check for coinfections from other tick-borne pathogens that the tick might also have injected. If one or more coinfections are present, they must be treated with additional medications. Some doctors recommend that patients with long-term Lyme disease, with or without coinfections, rebuild their immune systems with physical therapy, a special diet, and a coordinated plan designed to treat all symptoms and their causes.

ROCKY MOUNTAIN SPOTTED FEVER

The **microorganisms** that cause Rocky Mountain spotted fever (RMSF) are called *R. rickettsii*, a type of parasite. The rickettsii are named after Howard Ricketts, who identified the parasite in the early 1900s. Ticks pick up rickettsii from ground squirrels, snowshoe hares, voles, chipmunks, and other small mammals. Rickettsii can invade various types of cells, particularly the cells of blood vessels in muscle tissue. They also live inside the cells of developing tick eggs. Humans are accidental hosts who pass through territory where rickettsii-carrying ticks live.

Like many tick-borne illnesses, Rocky Mountain spotted fever has expanded beyond the region where it was first identified. The majority of reported cases now occur throughout the United States but mainly in Montana, some northeastern states, Tennessee, Georgia, and North and South Carolina. Rocky Mountain spotted fever has been on the rise since the 1990s as more people have moved into formerly undeveloped tick habitats. States report about five hundred cases a year of RMSF to the Centers for Disease Control (CDC), and the numbers are increasing.

This greatly magnified photo shows a tick searching for a feeding site on which to attach.

Around a week after a rickettsii-carrying tick bites a human, that person may develop a fever and possible flulike symptoms such as headaches, chills, nausea, and muscle aches and pains. Later, a rash may appear. When it does, it first appears on ankles and wrists, then spreads over the entire body.

An antibiotic in the tetracycline class should be given immediately, even before any test results come back. The medication should be taken for several days after the fever and other symptoms have completely gone away. This may take as

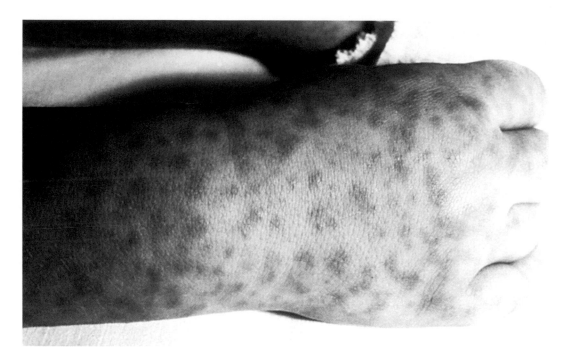

The rash associated with Rocky Mountain spotted fever was once called "black measles" because the disease was often a killer before antibiotics were used to treat it.

long as two weeks. If symptoms continue, then the patient should visit the doctor again to develop a plan for further, more intensive treatment.

Untreated, RMSF may cause damage in the liver, lungs, stomach, and kidneys. Other serious complications may include **meningitis**, heart attack, or **stroke.** Some people with severe cases of RMSF have suffered tissue damage that resulted in the loss of fingers and toes. Rocky Mountain spotted fever can be a killer in 25 percent of untreated cases and 5 percent of treated ones.

EHRLICHIOSIS

The discovery of two types of ehrlichiosis in the United States has been fairly recent. Researchers discovered one type in the 1980s and one in the 1990s. The lone star tick in south central and southeastern areas of the country spreads one kind. Both the black-legged tick and the dog tick spread the other type of ehrlichiosis. White-tailed deer are the favorite hosts of ehrlichiosis-carrying ticks. Humans traveling through areas infested with such ticks may get bitten and develop the disease. The number of humans who get the disease each year is not entirely clear. Most have been adult males over the age of

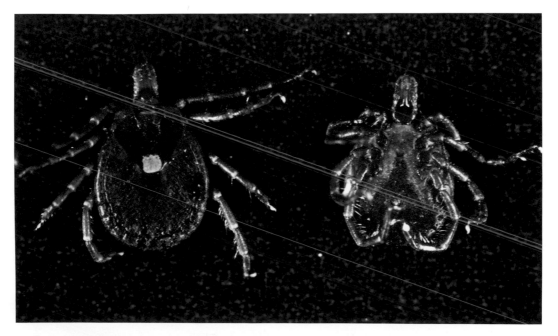

Ehrlichiosis-carrying lone star ticks can also carry and spread Lyme disease as well.

forty who spent time in outdoor activities between the months of April and September.

Symptoms of ehrlichiosis usually develop suddenly, five to ten days after a tick bite. Symptoms for all types of ehrlichiosis are similar to those of Rocky Mountain spotted fever—fever, headaches, chills, and nausea, all of which last for a couple of days. However, most adult patients do not develop a rash as they do with Rocky Mountain spotted fever. (About two-thirds of children with ehrlichiosis do get a rash, however.) Because the ticks that spread ehrlichiosis are the types that can also spread Lyme disease, sometimes they carry both diseases at the same time. Most patients get only mild illness with ehrlichiosis, which goes away on its own or with antibiotic treatment. However, the elderly, people who have weakened immune systems, or people who have had their spleen (an organ responsible for filtration of blood) removed, may develop more serious symptoms that require treatment in a hospital. Major organs, such as the heart, lung, and kidneys, may be affected. Other symptoms may include mental confusion, **coma**, and stroke.

TULAREMIA

Rabbit fever is the name once given to tularemia. However, researchers found that not just rabbits, but other wild animal species can carry tularemia bacteria. This group includes wild birds, cats, sheep, reptiles, and others. The most numerous

Dog ticks, often found in humid grassy or leafy areas, are difficult to control with pesticides.

carriers of the tularemia bacteria are wild mice, muskrats, beavers, voles, hares, and rabbits. The dog tick is the most common vector infecting humans. However, mosquitoes and deer flies may also spread the bacteria. The peak times of year for tularemia infection are in the summer and fall.

About half of the people who catch tularemia get it from a tick bite. Others can get it from handling skins of animals, particularly rabbit skins infected with the bacteria. Contaminated water and the bites or scratches of infected animals also spread tularemia. However, although tularemia is highly infectious, people cannot transmit the disease to one another.

Tularemia infects animals and humans in most parts of the

world except for tropical areas and the southern hemispheres. In North America, nearly forty-four states have reported tularemia cases, which average around two hundred cases per year from all causes. Arkansas, Missouri, and Oklahoma report about half of the cases. Children between the ages of five and nine, older people over seventy-five, and Native Americans of all ages make up the majority of reported cases. Fortunately, the incidence of this disease is declining.

Tularemia symptoms usually begin within a few days to one week after a tick bite. Symptoms may start with a fever, a sore at the bite site, and swollen lymph glands. In a severe form of tularemia, the victim may experience headaches, chills, and stomach pains. In other cases, patients may develop severe eye infections, sore throat, and pneumonia, which is a serious lung infection. Antibiotic treatment can clear up the disease completely. Fortunately, victims usually develop immunity to tularemia once they have had it.

TICK-BORNE RELAPSING FEVER

The soft-bodied, fast-feeding ticks that devour the blood of mice, rats, squirrels, and chipmunks are the vectors that spread the spirochete bacteria that cause tick-borne relapsing fever (TBRF) in humans. Most cases are found on other continents. However, in some mountainous areas of the western United States and Canada hundreds of tick-borne relapsing fever cases

have been reported to the CDC.
The soft ticks that transmit TBRF
to humans do so within thirty
minutes or so of feeding, usually
at nighttime. Victims have included tourists staying in old cottages
and cabins out West where small
mammal hosts nest or burrow.

Because the soft ticks feed
quickly and fall off, the victim
may wake up one morning
unaware of having been bitten
during the night. But a week or so
later, the trouble begins. Patients
with TBRF develop a high fever,
crushing headaches, severe muscle
and joint pain, nausea, chills, and
sweats. They may get purple spots
that indicate bleeding under the

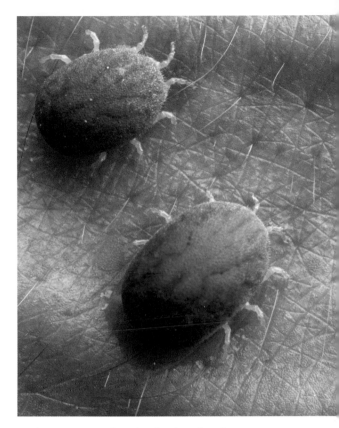

At least one outbreak of relapsing fever
originated in some of the Grand Canyon
tourist cabins in Arizona where soft ticks
were nesting.

skin. Their eyes may become extremely sensitive to light.
Organs may swell. Their heart rates may race. Some patients
develop nosebleeds and cough up blood. These symptoms can
last about three days before going away. However, the disease
is still lurking. The symptoms may start all over again a week
or two later, even with treatment. Without treatment, a patient

Only a small percentage of people enjoying the outdoors will ever develop a tick- borne illness. Most ticks bite other animals, not people.

may have three or more relapses and get all of the symptoms again as the spirochetes undergo changes. Tick-borne relapsing fever is treated with antibiotics such as erythromycin, tetracyclines, or penicillin.

BABESIOSIS

In the United States, both black-legged ticks and western black-legged ticks carry the parasite that causes babesiosis. Sometimes these ticks are carrying Lyme disease and babesiosis at the same time. The ticks pick up these parasites from animal hosts, mainly mice, then pass on the parasites when they feed on the blood of a human. Because the babesiosis parasites infect red blood cells, forty cases of babesiosis acquired through blood transfusions have been reported in the United States. Healthy people can carry the parasite silently without feeling sick, so there are probably many more cases than those reported—a couple of hundred each year, mainly in the

Mice and other small rodents are often the first infected hosts that ticks bite.

northeast and upper Midwest. In the elderly, in patients with weakened immune systems, and in patients without spleens, babesiosis causes symptoms resembling malaria, a serious disease that can be a killer. Babesiosis can have a long incubation period after a tick bites a human: anywhere from one to six weeks, several months, or even years. Symptoms in serious cases include a high fever, chills, fatigue, muscle pain, weight loss, blood infections, and death in 5 percent of the most severe cases of babesiosis. Some new types of antibiotics show promise in treating this illness.

3

THE HISTORY OF
TICK-BORNE ILLNESSES

More than 90 million years ago, gallons and gallons of yellow sap poured down the trunk of a huge tree and pooled at the bottom. All the organisms in its path got trapped in the goo. One of the organisms was a soft tick. Perhaps it lived in a nest or knothole in the tree and waited for a host to come home. But the sticky, flowing sap trapped the tick instead. It would never again gorge itself on another blood meal. In the millions of years that followed, the earth went through many cycles. The climate got hotter, colder, wetter, and drier. Over time, these forces turned the yellow sap into a kind of translucent orange-gold hard substance called amber weighing 80 pounds (36.3 kilograms). All those long-ago trapped organisms, including the tick, hardened into fossils, preserved imprints of the organisms, stuck in the amber.

Fast forward over 90 million years to the mid-1990s, when

Ancient fossils like this one can tell disease experts how long insects and disease-carrying ticks have been infecting animals, including humans.

someone discovered the 80-pound (36.3 kg) chunk of amber buried beneath a vacant lot in New Jersey. The American Museum of Natural History in New York City sent museum workers to carefully remove the amber from the surrounding earth. Back at the museum, scientists studied the amber and the ancient plants, animals, and the soft tick still trapped inside.

The researchers determined that the New Jersey tick was the oldest known soft tick ever found. The basic tick structures we see today that make ticks successful survivors were already in place millions of years ago when that tick was alive. Back then, no humans existed for ticks to feed on. Those two-legged hosts would come later. However, millions of years ago, there were plenty of other blood-filled vertebrates on which hungry ticks could feed.

When humans finally came along tens of thousands of years ago, ticks found new hosts. Prehistoric and ancient people probably began to catch tick-borne illnesses when they hunted wild animals in their habitats and later raised domesticated ones at home. These ancient people did not know that the blood-filled ticks they saw on these animals were making them sick. Some ancient people survived the tick-borne illnesses. Others did not.

Ignorance about the role of ticks in spreading diseases lasted for thousands of years, until the late 1800s. In 1893, two scientists, Theobald Smith and Fred Lucius Klibourne, discovered that tick vectors caused Texas cattle fever. This was a decade before other scientists would discover that mosquitoes and fleas also spread deadly diseases in animals and humans. Then, in 1903, the scientist J. E. Dutton discovered that the soft tick caused human cases of relapsing fever in the Congo. Dutton himself died of relapsing fever. Not long after, the scientist who discovered Rocky Mountain spotted fever died of a tick-borne disease. Soon experts began to study the feeding cycles of ticks as they consumed blood meals from host to host and spread disease in the process. Finding the source of the major tick-borne illness, Lyme disease, was a significant discovery in the 1970s.

LYME DISEASE

In 1975, in the small rural town of Old Lyme, Connecticut, a group of children developed arthritis. Not only that, but the doctors who treated them noticed that this development took place in late summer and early fall over several years. Many of the children, along with some adult members of their families, also got an odd pink rash that expanded into a circle. Scientists

African ticks like this one may infect local populations and travelers in southern parts of Africa and the West Indies.

and doctors soon paid close attention. Some studied research that described similar symptoms in European patients who had had tick-borne illnesses. The records went all the way back to the early 1900s. Researchers in the United States began to look at the ticks that local animals carried in the communities where the people were getting sick. They wondered if it was the same illness that was still fairly common in Europe. Sure enough, they identified a kind of tick that had bitten animals, usually white-footed mice and white-tailed deer, then bit humans, just as in the European cases. They called the American version of this illness Lyme disease, though it was not limited to Old Lyme, Connecticut. Within years, doctors learned of similar cases in other northeastern areas along the coast, in northern California, in Wisconsin, and in Minnesota.

In 1981, a researcher named Willy Burgdorfer identified the corkscrew-shaped spirochete bacteria that caused the disease. Once researchers knew what to look for, they discovered the same bacteria in museum specimens that dated back to the 1800s and early 1900s. The researchers guessed that the disease probably existed even earlier than that. However, it was limited during the early centuries of the United States. Settlers had cut down forests and also hunted deer, the primary tick hosts of the Lyme disease spirochete. When the woodlands began to grow back, the deer population rebounded. As a result, farmers and townspeople were living closer to nearby

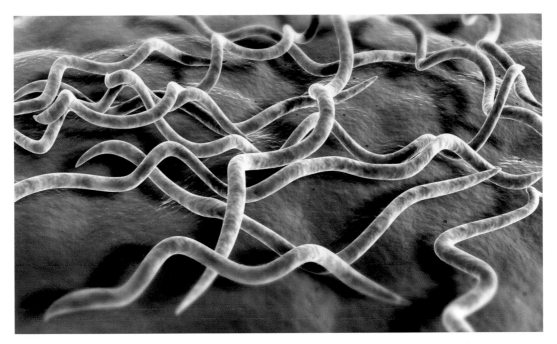

Lyme disease bacteria, called spirochetes, have curly, spiral shapes.

deer. Soon, the ticks made the jump to humans. Today, Lyme disease is a problem wherever humans have moved into areas that include deer habitats.

ROCKY MOUNTAIN SPOTTED FEVER

Knowledge about tick-borne illnesses was almost nonexistent in the late 1800s. So when there was an outbreak of a disease in the Snake River Valley in Idaho in 1896, people thought the rash that came with it was a type of measles. In fact, they called the frightening illness black measles. Hundreds of people

41

Howard Ricketts, the first researcher to identify Rocky Mountain spotted fever as a tick-borne illness, died from a microorganism similar to that of RMSF.

in the area came down with this dreaded disease. Many of them died. The disease spread north to Washington State and Montana as well as south and west to Arizona, New Mexico, and California. The disease was so serious, the government founded the Rocky Mountain Laboratory in Hamilton, Montana, to study the illness. Howard Ricketts was the first researcher to identify the disease as a tick-borne illness. Prior to the discovery of effective medications in the 1940s, more than 30 percent of RMSF victims died from it.

EHRLICHIOSIS

As tick-borne illness discoveries go, ehrlichiosis illnesses in humans were latecomers. In 1953, researchers identified the first human case in the world in Japan. Identification of the two ehrlichiosis species that cause human infections in the United States also came late. Sidney A. Ewing, a veterinary researcher studying tick-borne illnesses in dogs, isolated one ehrlichiosis species in 1970. Researchers discovered the other in the 1980s. However, it was not until 1999 that the infection named after Ewing was reported in a human. Scientists are still studying ehrlichiosis. The disease seems to be spreading. The illness can occur in almost any area of the United States, as well as in many foreign countries. It mainly affects people whose immune systems have been weakened by other diseases.

TULAREMIA

Drinking contaminated water, handling rabbit skins, and being bitten by deer flies caused most cases of tularemia worldwide

Francisella tularensis **is the name of the bacterium that causes tularemia. Ticks that bite rabbits, hares, and rodents infected with the bacteria may go on to infect other animals, including humans.**

Ticks and Pets

....

Throughout history, tick-borne illnesses have infected animals that humans hunted or raised as livestock. The most significant jump of infected ticks onto humans probably took place after ticks attached themselves to sheep, goats, horses, and cattle. Livestock today continue to develop tick-borne illnesses along with the humans who raise them.

House pets, such as dogs and cats, are also tick hosts. Dogs get Lyme disease from the ticks that carry the spirochete bacteria. Dogs also develop the arthritic symptoms that people get. Symptoms that show a dog may be infected with a tick-borne illness include lameness, swollen joints, fatigue, and poor appetite. Treatment is usually the same as that for humans—antibiotics for at least three weeks or more. Because cats groom themselves constantly, ticks have a harder time attaching to them. This is not good news for their human companions, however. When outdoor cats flick away ticks inside the house, the hungry ticks are on the loose indoors. The very next host likely to appear is a human. Various treatments are available to rid a house of both fleas and ticks.

Pet owners can take various preventive steps to keep their pets from getting bitten by a tick. Tick collars and certain medications that can be rubbed into fur help keep ticks away from dogs and cats during tick season. In addition, dogs and cats should not be allowed to roam freely through tick-infested woods and meadows during tick season. People should check their pets daily after the animals have been outdoors. Grooming a pet every day is a great way to keep ticks from being attached for very long on a pet.

House pets that go outdoors should get tick checks and grooming whenever they come indoors during tick season.

throughout history. However, in 1966, the first of three out-breaks of tick-borne tularemia occurred in the United States. Native American children who had played with dogs infected by dog ticks were the primary victims. The Pine Ridge and Rosebud Indian reservations in South Dakota reported twelve cases. Twelve more cases occurred in 1979 on the Crow Indian Reservation in Montana. Then, in 1984, twenty or more cases broke out in the Crow Creek and Lower Brule Indian reservations in South Dakota. Tularemia-carrying ticks likely infected small wild animals and pet dogs living on reservation lands. With many four-legged hosts available, the dog ticks that carried tularemia probably thrived on the reservations and eventually attached themselves to children passing through the tick-infested area.

TICK-BORNE RELAPSING FEVER

Tick-borne relapsing fever has been around since ancient times. TBRF follows an unusual pattern. The patient develops symptoms, which last for about two to eight days, and then go away. The symptoms can return several times throughout the victim's life. Because its relapsing pattern may hold clues to the operations of the human immune system, many researchers today are interested in studying this disease, even though it is uncommon. Perhaps **antibodies** cause symptoms to go away but cannot completely fight off the disease all at once.

BABESIOSIS

Some historians believe that a babesiosis-like disease that afflicted domestic animals is mentioned in the Bible. In the late 1800s, researchers identified the babesiosis parasite. However, the disease was thought of as one that infected animals, not the humans who raised them. This changed in 1957 when a cattle farmer in Europe was infected with babesiosis. Babesiosis has also infected people in the United States, where there have been several hundred cases reported since the 1980s.

The fight against tick-borne diseases is not yet over. Old tick-borne illnesses such as tularemia have decreased over time. However, new tick-borne illnesses continue to emerge as humans and their animals move into tick territories around the world.

4

LIVING WITH A
TICK—BORNE ILLNESS

Ticks have had 90 million years to develop their effective bloodthirsty, disease-spreading ways. But humans can catch up. Preventing tick bites greatly decreases the chances that a person will ever have to cope with a tick-borne illness. Tick avoidance is a first step. Public health officials have made efforts to decrease host populations, such as allowing deer hunting. In addition, researchers have developed various **vaccines** that help prevent some tick-borne diseases in domestic animals. However, vaccines for preventing tick-borne illnesses in humans are still fairly experimental.

Self-help remains the best way to prevent tick bites. People who love the outdoors should know where and when ticks hang out and which ticks are the biggest troublemakers in their area. The number of tick-borne illnesses that get reported to the Centers for Disease Control are probably much lower than actual

Time to roll down sleeves and pants and apply insect repellent!

cases. The CDC points out that the numbers reported for all tick-borne illnesses each year could possibly be doubled or tripled, because of all the cases that go unreported. Deaths from tick-borne illnesses, while frightening, are so rare that when they happen, they usually make headlines.

- In 2000, the Centers for Disease Control said that twelve states accounted for 95 percent of the 16,877 reported Lyme disease cases that year. These states included Connecticut, Rhode Island, New Jersey, New York, Delaware, Pennsylvania, Massachusetts, Maryland, Wisconsin, Minnesota, New Hampshire and Vermont.

Preventing Tick Bites

....

Tick territories are located in grassy areas, on leaf-littered forest floors, and in sandy, dusty areas. Where there is one tick, there are probably thousands of them nearby. They sense someone approaching even if you do not know they are around! Ticks hear your footsteps and can measure the carbon dioxide in your breath. They are waiting for you, or your dog, or nearby deer, field mice, cows, birds, and other animals to supply them with their next meal. To prevent them from feasting on you, here are some tips to make sure they do not get attached to you:

- Wear light-colored socks and pants during tick season from spring to fall.
- Tuck pants into boots or socks.
- Spray insect repellent on pant legs, shoes, and boots. Experts recommend permethrin or DEET, though not both together. Without repellent, ticks can travel toward the upper parts of your body to your neck or head to find exposed skin. If one attaches itself to your scalp, it will be difficult to spot the tick.
- Walk in the middle of the paths through the woods so as not to brush against bushes and other plant life where ticks may be hiding.
- Avoid rolling around in grass, dirt, or sand if you are in tick territories during the tick season.
- Do tick checks after arriving home. It is easier to feel a tick when shampooing hair. Check head, neck, and ears then.

Most ticks thrive in damp places, such as grassy areas and leaf-covered forest floors.

Rocky Mountain spotted fever is second to Lyme disease in causing tick-borne illness. The CDC lists 250–1,200 reported cases a year from all states except Hawaii, Vermont, Maine, and Alabama. The states of Delaware, Maryland, Washington, D.C., Virginia, West Virginia, North Carolina, South Carolina, Oklahoma, and Florida account for 50 percent of reported cases. Of those, 35 percent occurred in North Carolina and Oklahoma. The ticks that cause RMSF are active between April and August.

- Ehrlichiosis cases number approximately 150–200 annually, according to the CDC. The majority of cases occur in Arkansas, Florida, Georgia, Missouri, North Carolina, Oklahoma, Tennessee, Texas, and Virginia. However, a small number of cases have been reported in most other states. The lone star tick that causes ehrlichiosis is active between April and September, with June and July the most active months.

- Tularemia accounts for about two hundred cases of tick-borne illness reported to the CDC yearly. About half of those cases are caused by tick bites. Most tick-borne tularemia cases have occurred in south-central and western areas, particularly in South and North Dakota, Arkansas, Missouri, and Oklahoma in the spring to late summer months.

- Only about twenty-five cases of tick-borne relapsing fever are reported to the CDC each year. These occur mainly in the summertime. A number of those cases have been associated with people who had slept in rustic cabins where small animals nest and where soft ticks often live.

- Several hundred babesiosis cases have been reported since the disease was discovered in 1957—a handful per year. However, each year there are increasing numbers of reported cases. Most of them occur on islands off coastal Massachusetts, Rhode Island, and Connecticut.

KNOW THE SYMPTOMS

Unfortunately, getting the test results for most tick-borne illnesses takes a long time. However, since some untreated tick-borne illnesses can cause serious problems, or even death, doctors often begin treatment right away. A doctor will suspect a tick-borne illness if the patient:

- has a sudden, unexplained fever that lasts more than a day, if it is accompanied by mental confusion and breathing problems.
- has not responded to antibiotics. This may indicate a tick-borne virus is making the patient sick.

Removing a Tick

Equipment: Tweezers
(optional) magnifier or magnification glasses
soap, water, antibiotic cream

Instructions: Ask a parent to help you remove the tick. Do not use matches, nail polish, nail polish remover, petroleum jelly, or other substances to remove or suffocate a tick. These substances *do not work* and may cause the tick to release more of its pathogens into you.

Look closely at the tick to locate its mouthparts (with a magnifier or magnification glasses if available). Line up the points of the tweezers near the mouthparts where the tick is attached. Pull gently at the mouthparts—not the tick's body—until it is dislodged. Wash the bite with soap, rinse the area, and dry it off. Apply antibiotic cream.

Save the tick in a plastic bag labeled with the date you removed the tick. If you develop symptoms later, bring in the tick, which can be tested.

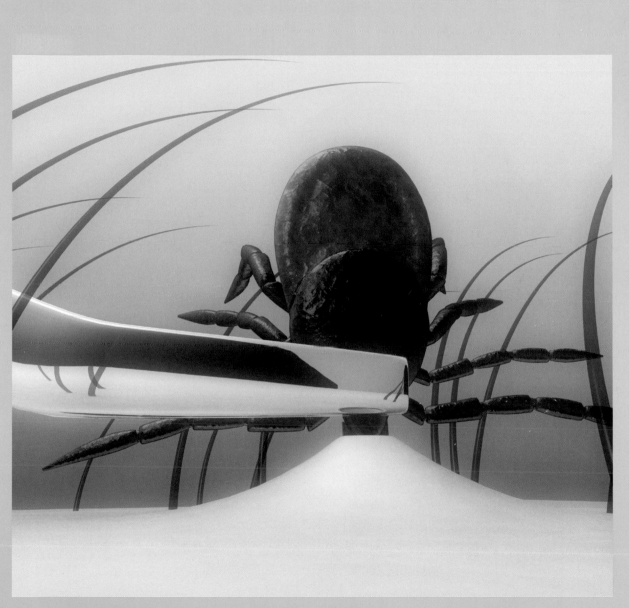

Use a magnifying glass to locate a tick's mouthparts. Then use tweezers to pull the mouthparts from the skin.

A tick-borne illness should be suspected whenever someone who has been in tick-infested areas develops a fever, along with chills, a headache, and especially a rash.

- has spent the previous thirty days outdoors during tick season in areas where ticks are active.
- has a weakened immune system; has had his or her spleen removed, or is elderly.
- lives in a state where there is a high incidence of certain tick-borne illnesses.
- is a farmer, rancher, outdoor guide or ranger, hunter, hiker, landscaper, gardener, boater, or fisherman.
- is a child who lives in a tick-infested area.
- has a rash, headaches, muscle aches, or chills with a fever.

Most people, even those who spend a great deal of time outdoors, will never be bitten by an infected tick. As efficient as these ancient creatures are at getting a blood meal, ticks prefer other animals to humans when they go out to eat. People should not avoid the outdoors in order to avoid ticks. Instead, take simple preventive steps when going outdoors into tick territory to prevent ticks from latching on. If a tick does climb aboard, doing regular tick checks can rob a tick of the time it needs to inject a disease.

GLOSSARY

antibiotic—A medication that can cure some diseases caused by bacteria and other microorganisms.

antibodies—The white blood cells that the body's immune system creates to defend against disease-causing microorganisms.

arachnid—A group of multilegged biting organisms such as spiders, ticks, scorpions, and mites.

babesiosis—A tick-borne illness caused by a parasite, and which affects red blood cells.

bacteria—Microorganisms that often cause disease; germs.

coma—A state of deep unconsciousness.

ehrlichiosis—A tick-borne illness caused by certain types of bacteria.

habitat—The home or environment in which an organism lives.

host—A cell or organism that is taken over by another organism such as a tick or parasite.

hypostome—The hooked mouthpart a tick uses to drill into a host and to drink its blood.

immune system—The body's system for fighting a disease caused by foreign substances.

incubation period—The period of time between exposure to an infection and the appearance of the first symptoms of illness.

infection—Illness caused when harmful bacteria, viruses, parasites, or certain other germs enter the body.

larva—The first stage of a tick's life after it is hatched from an egg.

Lyme disease—A tick-borne illness caused by an infected black-legged tick that carries spirochete bacteria.

meningitis—A disease that causes swelling in the covering of the brain.

microorganism—A tiny organism visible only through a microscope.

neurological—Having to do with the brain, spine, and nerves in the body.

nymph—The second stage of a tick's life after it feeds as a larva.

parasites—Organisms that live or reproduce by feeding off a live host organism.

pathogens—Harmful organisms that can cause disease.

questing—The movements of ticks' legs as they prepare to jump onto a host passing nearby.

Rocky Mountain spotted fever (RMSF)—A tick-borne illness caused by the rickettsii bacterium.

spirochetes—Corkscrew-shaped bacteria involved in Lyme disease and tick-borne relapsing fever, among other tick-borne illnesses.

stroke—A weakness or unconsciousness that results from a burst or blocked blood vessel in the brain.

symptoms—The body's signals that an illness or injury is present.

tick—A blood-feeding arachnid.

tick-borne relapsing fever (TBRF)—The only tick-borne illness that a soft tick causes in humans.

tularemia—A type of tick-borne illness caused by bacteria that some mammals such as rabbits, moles, and mice carry.

vaccine—A type of preventive medication to keep a disease from developing.

vectors—Disease-spreading organisms such as ticks and mosquitoes.

vertebrate—A bony animal, reptile, or fish with a spine.

virus—A harmful particle that invades some of an organism's cells in order to reproduce and which causes illness.

FIND OUT MORE

Organizations

Lyme Disease Association, Inc.
P.O. Box 1438
Jackson, NJ 08527
888-366-6611
http://www.lymediseaseassociation.org

Lyme Disease Foundation
P.O. Box 332
Tolland, CT 06084-0332
800-886-5963
http://www.lyme.org

Books

Drummond, Roger, Ph.D. *Ticks and What You Can Do About Them*. Berkeley, CA: Wilderness Press, 2004.

Harris, Monica. *Tick* (Bug Book). Chicago, IL: Heinemann, 2003.

Hirschmann, Kris. *Ticks* (Parasites). San Diego, CA: Kidhaven Press, 2004.

Kravetz, Jonathan. *Ticks* (Gross Bugs). New York, NY: Rosen Publishing Group's PowerKids Press, 2006.

Somervill, Barbara A. *Ticks: Digging for Blood*. New York, NY: Rosen Publishing Group, Incorporated, 2008.

Vanderhoof-Forschner, Karen. *Everything You Need to Know About Lyme Disease and Other Tick-Borne Disorders*. 2nd Edition E-Book, New York, NY: John Wiley & Sons, Inc. 2004.

Web Sites

Resources and support groups for patients with Lyme disease.
http://www.lymenet.org
http://www.lymealliance.org

ABOUT THE AUTHOR

L. H. Colligan writes about many topics, from study skills to activity books and children's fiction. Although she lives and regularly hikes and picnics in tick territory in Westchester County, New York, she has never had Lyme disease. Prior to writing this book, she did not know that ticks had such clever ways to get a meal. Now, she will be more vigilant with tick prevention methods.

INDEX

Page numbers for illustrations are in **boldface**

adults, tick-borne illnesses in, **10,** 24, 29–30
adult stage ticks, 14, **15,** 22
African ticks, **39**
amber, 36–37
American dog tick, **12**
animals, as hosts, 12–14, **13,** 16–19, 26, 30–31, 33, **34,** 38, 57
    See also individual animals
antibiotics, 11, 21, 24, 27, 30, 32, 35, 44, 53
arachnids, 13
Argasidae. See soft ticks

babesiosis, 22, 34–35, 47, 53
bacteria, 16, 20, 21, 26, 31, **43**
birds, as hosts, 14, 18, 19, 50
bites, tick, 9, 11–13, 20, 27, 29, 35, 48, 50, 52
black-legged hard ticks, 20, 22–24, **23,** 29, 34
black measles. *See* Rocky Mountain spotted fever (RMSF)
blood, feeding on, 9, 12–18, 20–21, 33, 34, 38
Burgdorfer, Willy, 40

cats, as hosts, 44
checking for ticks, 50, 57
chemicals, tick-injected, 20–21
children, tick-borne illnesses in, 7, **10,** 11, 24, 30, 32, 46, **56,** 57

deaths, 7, 11, 28, 35, 49, 53
deer, as hosts, 19, 23, 29, 40–41, 48, 50
deer flies, 31, 43
digging in, 19, 20–21
disease-spreading process, 12–19, 22, 31, 32, 38–39
dogs, as hosts, 42, 44, **45,** 46, 50
dog ticks, 29, 31, **31**
Dutton, J. E., 38

ehrlichiosis, 22, **29,** 29–30, 42–43, 52
elderly people, tick-borne illnesses in, 30, 32, 35
Ewing, Sidney A., 42–43

fleas, 38, 44
fossils, 36–37, **37**
Francisella tularensis, **43**

habitats, tick, 13–14, **31,** 50, **51,** 53
Haller's organ, **17,** 17–18
hard ticks, 13, 14, **14,** 20, 22–24, **23,** 29, 34
hosts, 14, 17, 23, 40–41, 48
    See also animals, as hosts
humans, as hosts, 12, 18–19, 22, 24, 26, **34,** 38, 44
hypostomes. *See* mouthparts

immune systems, 18, 20, 26, 30, 35, 43, 46, 57
incubation periods, 21, 35
insect repellents, 50
Ixodidae. See hard ticks

Klibourne, Fred Lucius, 38

larva stage ticks, 14, 22
life-cycle forms, 14–15, 22
livestock, as hosts, 19, 44, 47, 48, 50
lone star ticks, 29, **29,** 52
Lyme disease, **21,** 22–26, **23, 24, 29,** 30, 34, 39–41, **41,** 44, 52

malaria, 35
males, tick-borne illnesses in, 24, 29–30
mating practices, 15
medications. *See* antibiotics; treatments
mice, as hosts, 20, 22, 23, 34, **35,** 40, 50
mosquitoes, 16, 31, 38
mouthparts, 20, **20,** 54, **55**

Native Americans, tick-borne illnesses in,
    32, 46
New Jersey ticks, 37–38
nymph stage ticks, 14, **15,** 22

parasites, 17, 26, 27, 34, 47
pathogens, 16, 19, 26
prevention, 7, **8,** 44, **45,** 48–50, **49,** 57

questing behavior, **16,** 17, **17**, 20, **27**

R. rickettsii parasite, 26, 27
rabbit fever. *See* tularemia
rabbits, as hosts, **19**
rashes, 30, **56,** 57
    delayed, 7, 9, 10, 20, 21
    Lyme disease, **21,** 24, **24,** 39
    Rocky Mountain spotted fever, 27,
        28, 41
removing ticks, 54, **55**
Ricketts, Howard, 26, 42, **42**
Rocky Mountain spotted fever (RMSF),
    6–7, 9–11, **10,** 22, 26–28, **28,** 30, 38,
    41–42, 52

saliva, tick, 19, **20,** 20–21
seasons, tick, 22, 31, 53
Smith, Theobald, 38
soft ticks, 13–14, 17, 32–33, **33,** 36–38
spirochetes bacteria, 20–21, 24, 32–34,
    40, **41,** 44
spleens, absence of, 30, 35, 57
states, ticks found in, 7, 22, 27, 32, 40,
    46, 49, 52

statistics, 22–23, 27, 46, 48–49, 52–53
symptoms, 6, 18–21, 53, **56,** 57
    See also specific illnesses

teenagers, tick-borne illnesses in, **10,** 24
tetracycline, 11, 27, 34
Texas cattle fever, 38
tick-borne relapsing fever (TBRF), 14, 22,
    32–34, **33,** 38, 46, 53
ticks, 7, **12,** 12–19, **16, 17, 18, 20, 27,**
    37
    See also hard ticks; soft ticks
treatments, 11, 21, 24, 26–28, 30, 33–35,
    44, 53
tularemia, **19,** 22, 30–32, 43, **43,** 46, 47,
    52

vaccines, 48
vectors, 16, 22, 31, 32, 38
vertebrates, 12–13, 38

western black-legged ticks, 34